AN ACT OF COURAGE

One dark night the Ku Klux Klan, its members wearing white sheets and carrying blazing torches, visited the school. They looked like ghosts coming up the steps of a building.

They didn't like the way Mary had been telling the Negroes to vote. The Klansmen thought they could scare her but they didn't know her very well. She stood on the steps, between two white pillars, and faced them. She wore a long flowing cape. Light from the hall shone out on her. Every window was lighted. In the building, the choir she had trained was practicing. Eighty men from the Ku Klux Klan faced her.

"If you keep teaching these people of yours they can vote, we'll burn your buildings. "

Mrs. Bethune was very angry but she said quietly, "If you burn them, I'll build them up again."

SHE WANTED TO READ:
The Story of Mary McLeod Bethune
was originally published by Abingdon Press.

Critics' Corner:

"[Mrs. Bethune] became a famous and distinguished woman —a college president, doctor of humanities and friend of the late President Roosevelt....The book is simply written yet effective in telling its story."   —*Chicago News*

"...a well-paced version. It should be useful in all libraries, particularly school libraries...."   —*School Library Journal*

Also recommended by: Bro-Dart Foundation, Elementary School Library Collection.

About the Author and Illustrator:

ELLA KAISER CARRUTH was born in Cleveland, Ohio. She attended public schools there, and was graduated (A.B.) from Smith College in Northampton, Massachusetts. She is a past president of the trustees of Kirkland Town Library, Clinton, New York, where she lived for many years when her husband was a professor at Hamilton College. Mrs. Carruth now lives in Winter Park, Florida. She has written for magazines and newspapers, but SHE WANTED TO READ: *The Story of Mary McLeod Bethune* is her first book.

HERBERT MCCLURE is a native of North Carolina, but he now lives in Long Island and has a studio in New York City. He has illustrated books and also magazines, such as *Redbook* and *Good Housekeeping*.

She Wanted to Read

THE STORY OF MARY McLEOD BETHUNE

By Ella Kaiser Carruth

ILLUSTRATED BY HERBERT McCLURE

AN ARCHWAY PAPERBACK

WASHINGTON SQUARE PRESS • NEW YORK

SHE WANTED TO READ:

The Story of Mary McLeod Bethune

Archway Paperback edition published October, 1969

L

Published by Washington Square Press,
a division of Simon & Schuster, Inc., 630 Fifth Avenue, New York, N.Y.

WASHINGTON SQUARE PRESS editions are distributed in the
U.S. by Simon & Schuster, Inc., 630 Fifth Avenue, New
York, N.Y. 10020 and in Canada by Simon & Schuster
of Canada, Ltd., Richmond Hill, Ontario, Canada.

3 4 5 2 1 0

To my father who
fought for freedom

One

Mary Jane McLeod was ten years old. She was long-legged and pig-tailed. Her grandmother, who lived with the family, said, "She's no-wise pretty, but she's strong as a mule." This was a perfect description of the little Negro girl.

Mary was the fifteenth of seventeen children. They all worked in the cotton fields. She had to be strong to do her share of the work—and she worked swiftly. She was the champion cotton-picker in the family.

The children's parents worked in the fields too. Their names were Sam and Patsy. Patsy, besides picking cotton, did all the cooking for her large family. Often she did washing for a white family that lived in a big white house half a mile away.

On Saturday she delivered the clean clothes in a basket balanced on her head. She was tall and straight, and she walked like a queen.

One Saturday Patsy let Mary go with her to carry extra packages. Mary loved to go places with her mother. They always had happy times, talking and singing together on the hot South Carolina roads.

While she waited for her mother to come out of the big house, Mary looked at a playhouse in the yard. It belonged to the two little daughters of the white woman. Soon they came out and invited Mary in.

The playhouse was big enough for all three children. They played "ladies" and Mary Jane pretended that she was nurse-maid for the beautiful doll. She sat rocking the doll, and then she noticed a book on the table and she wanted to touch it and look at it. She picked it up and had just peeked inside when one of the little girls screamed at her, "Put that down!"

"I just want to feel it," said Mary. "I just want—"

"Put it down!" the other sister cried.

"I won't hurt it," Mary said softly. She was so puzzled and hurt at their cross words that she nearly cried.

"Books are for people who can read. You can't read." The girls seemed upset.

Mary put the book down and set the doll in her chair. Then she rushed out of the house. On the gravel driveway she

met her mother and as they started back over the hot road, she sobbed out her story, jabbing her bare toes into the scratchy sand.

Patsy held her head high to the sun. She had once been a slave but her ancestors in Africa had been royal people. They had been rulers in a matriarchy. Patsy had explained to Mary that this was a tribe where women, not men, were the chiefs. To be sure, Patsy did not rule a tribe in America, but what she said was law in the McLeod family, and that family was almost big enough to be called a tribe. Patsy wished she knew how to spell out words, but she said she was too old to learn. She now looked down tenderly at her small daughter.

Squeezing her mother's hand till it hurt, Mary cried, "I *will* learn to read."

"I hope so," said her mother.

"Don't *hope* so, *know* so," pleaded Mary.

Patsy hugged her little daughter. "Your old Granny *knows* so," she said. "Granny told Sam that you were just bound to read. 'That child's just bent on amounting to something,' she said."

"You think she's right?"

"Don't you?" Patsy asked.

"I know so, like Granny said."

Mary's father, Sam, couldn't read. He had been a slave before the War Between the States. Patsy and Sam had belonged to different masters, both of whom were kind men. When Sam told Mr. McLeod, his master, he wanted to marry Patsy, Mr. McLeod said, "I'll find out what it will cost to buy her. But you'll have to earn the money yourself."

Sam was a field hand who loved working on the land. To earn money to buy Patsy he was willing to do anything. He worked after hours in a lumber mill. He saved every penny. After two years he took the money he had saved to his mas-

8

ter and asked him to buy her for him. Mr. McLeod bought Patsy. He allowed the couple to be married on his plantation. He even gave Sam one of his own suits for a wedding suit.

Sam and Patsy lived in a little four-room cabin on the McLeod plantation. There many of their seventeen children were born while Sam and Patsy were still slaves. These children were born slaves.

Mary Jane was born later, in 1875, after Abraham Lincoln freed all slaves. Her parents were free, so Mary was born a free child. She was just as free as any white girls. Yet she couldn't do many things they could do. Worst of all, she couldn't read.

Mary spent long hot hours in the fields picking cotton with her brothers and sisters. The other children seemed satisfied, but as Mary picked row after row, she chanted, "I want to read. I want to read. I have to go to school to learn to read. Please, dear God, let me go to school."

Mary could pick 250 pounds of cotton a day. Even her brothers couldn't do better than that. The cotton was fluffy and light, but it made many loads for a little girl. On one trip to carry a sack chock full of cotton to the cabin, Mary was surprised to see a stranger watching her.

"I'm Miss Wilson," the lady said.

"*Miss* Wilson!" Mary had never heard a colored woman called Miss or Mrs. On South Carolina plantations they were always called by their first names—Patsy or Mary or Jane.

"*Miss* Wilson." Mary liked that. It sounded so respectable. She made up her mind that some day she would be called *Miss* McLeod. And if she ever got married, she'd be *Mrs.* Somebody.

Mary wasn't accustomed to talking with strangers and she wished either her father or her mother were in sight.

"Just a minute," she said. "Here comes my mother." Sam and Patsy both came from the field when they saw the strange lady.

Mary said, "This is Miss Wilson."

"Welcome, Miss Wilson," Patsy said. "Can we do something for you?"

"I hope so," Miss Wilson said. "The Presbyterian Mission Board in the North has sent me down here. They want me to start a school for Negro children in Mayesville. We'd like children from every family. I hope some of yours can go."

Patsy thought a minute. "There's so much work to be done, we couldn't spare but one."

"Yes," said Sam. "We could only let one of them go."

Mary held her breath and wondered if she would be the one.

Sam and Patsy both looked at Mary. Finally Patsy said, "Our Mary's sort of different. I guess she ought to be the one to go."

Samuel said, "She's homely, but she's smart."

11

Mary let out a sigh of relief. "Am I going to *read?*" she asked.

Miss Wilson smiled, "Yes, you will learn to read."

Mary fell on her knees and whispered, "Thank you, God."

Miss Wilson smiled at the parents. Mary picked up her empty gunny sack and hurried back to the cotton field. She filled the sack as fast as she could pick and emptied it and filled it again. She felt that every full bag brought her a little nearer to the day when she could read. The girls' words, "*You* can't read," rang in her ears. They still hurt. But Miss Wilson's words made her determined.

She flipped the fluffy white cotton bolls into the gunny sack.

"I'm gonna read!"

After supper she often put her hand on the Bible that lay on the table in the McLeod cabin. It was a present from their pastor. It was the only book in their home. Nobody could read it but everybody loved it. Softly Mary said, "Soon I will read you, blessed book."

Two

A few days before Mary started to school, her father bought her a present. Usually there wasn't enough money to buy anyone a present. But Sam said this was a very special time. One of his children was going to school. He asked Mary what she wanted. "Something to write with," she said. She was thinking of a pencil. But she got something better—a piece of chalk to write with and a slate to write on.

The next day, with her precious slate and chalk, she started the dusty walk to school. Her bright red gingham dress was starched so stiffly it stuck out straight. Her black hair was braided in little pigtails and each one was tied with a tiny red bow. Her shoes had metal tips to keep them from scuffing and were heavy on her feet. It was a long, five-mile walk to school.

But what did that matter? At the door was Miss Wilson. She would teach Mary so that no one would ever again say, "You can't read!" Mary Jane McLeod was beginning her education.

After school Mary walked the five miles home. After supper the family gathered around the table. The other children were curious. "Now you've been to school, Mary. Teach us how to read!"

Mary laughed, "You are crazy! I can't learn to read in one day!"

Mary didn't care that her school was a

poor one-room building. The benches were hard. Sometimes their jagged edges hurt her legs. She didn't complain. She just wiggled a little and changed her position. On cold days in the winter her eyes smarted from the smoke of the pot-bellied stove. The stove couldn't quite burn up the pine cones that were stuffed into it. When she got to school on frosty mornings, she was glad to stretch her hands out to it. Sometimes, even though she had run and jumped all the way to school, she was cold clear through her gingham dress. Miss Wilson would take her hands between her own warm hands and say, "I can't let my most faithful pupil freeze."

It wasn't long before Mary could read the Bible.

Soon after that she learned to use figures. She could count. She studied arithmetic and was happy when she could help her father figure. She also helped the neighbors and sometimes kept them from being cheated. They thought that was better than just reading.

When Mary started her second school year, the little one-room building was no longer in use. There was a new yellow brick school that had two rooms. It was called Mayesville Institute. Miss Wilson loved it and so did Mary.

It too had a pot-bellied stove that smoked. But it had desks and chairs instead of benches. Mary's desk and chair didn't fit her very well. The desk was too low and the chair was too high. She had to bend over like a crook-neck squash when she wrote, but she didn't mind. She was happy to be able to write.

The school had no blackboard, so Miss Wilson and her pupils painted big pieces of cardboard black. The children put colored paper flowers around the edges of the windows. They hung their own gay colored drawings on the walls. It was a bright little school.

In the yard were rope swings. The

screaming children gave each other high, run-under pushes at recess time.

Mary was in her third year at school when something happened that made her father strut with pride about his daughter.

One Sunday, right after dinner, two white men rode up to the McLeod's cabin door.

"Hope there's no trouble," Patsy whispered. Sometimes white men riding up to a Negro's cabin did mean trouble.

Sure enough, there was trouble—but not for Sam and Patsy. The white men needed help.

They said to Sam, "We heard your Mary can figure. Can she?"

"She can. Why you ask?"

"We think we're being cheated. We'd like for Mary to figure our accounts and see."

Sam called Mary. She said she'd try. She looked at the papers the white men had brought. She studied the columns of figures. They were being cheated.

Miss Wilson was very proud when she heard about the incident.

Mary was fifteen years old when Miss Wilson said she couldn't teach her any more. Mary had gone as far as she could in the little yellow brick school house. At the end of the school year, she graduated. Her class was the first to be graduated from Mayesville Institute.

What a different looking girl Mary was from the eleven-year-old who had begun school in a red gingham dress and heavy shoes. On Commencement Day Mary wore a lovely white dress and white shoes and stockings.

For Mary's dress, Patsy had saved all her laundry money. Sam had managed to save a little here and there. Grandma surprised them with money for the white shoes and stockings. When they asked her where she got it, she smiled mischievously and patted a deep pocket hidden in one of her many petticoats.

Every child was well dressed for the occasion. Their beloved teacher, Miss Wilson, dressed in her best, sat facing them. On either side of her sat the speakers, some black, some white. After the speech, each child recited a little piece.

Then came the big moment for Mary. A diploma, tied with a white ribbon, was put into her hands. She held it lovingly. It proved she could read.

Three

The next day Mary went back to the cotton field with her brothers and sisters. She hoped to work hard enough to earn money to go to school again. Her father wanted to give her a little after the cotton crop was sold if that were possible. He wasn't sure.

Before the year's crop was even planted, a great loss came to the family. As the ground was being plowed for the

cotton planting, their one mule, Old
Bush, fell down in front of the plow.

The family couldn't get him up. Mary
patted him. She remembered how she
used to ride astride his back when she
was only five years old. Sam ran his hand
over Old Bush's neck.

"Mule's dead," Sam told his family.

Mary's hopes of more schooling died
too. No mule, no plowing; no plowing, no
cotton crop; no crop, no money; no money, no school. Mary buried her face in
Old Bush's mane and cried.

One of her brothers strapped the har-
ness around his waist and started to pull
the plow. It was such hard pulling that
one boy couldn't do much at a time. The
others took turns. Mary was glad she was
"strong as a mule," as her grandmother
had said. The McLeods would have to
have a new mule as soon as possible. That
meant there might never be any more
money for Mary's schooling.

"Please, Lord, let me go to school some

more," Mary prayed as she pulled the plow.

For the second time Miss Wilson brought Mary's answer. Mary saw her hurrying down the road, waving something in her hand. Patsy and Mary went to meet her. She was carrying a letter. She hugged Mary around the shoulders and said, "Mary, you can go to school again."

Mary stared at her. Patsy said, "But there's no money."

"This letter says there is!"

"Tell us," said Patsy.

"Out in Denver, Colorado, there is a dressmaker named Mary Chrissman. She believes in freedom and education for all Negroes. Her father would have fought for it in the War Between the States if he hadn't been a Quaker. Most Quakers will not fight, so he wasn't in the army. But he did go south to teach Negroes to read and write. He told his daughter about it when she was a little girl. Now she wants to carry on his work."

"How?" asked Patsy.

"By tithing."

Mary looked puzzled. "What's tithing?"

"It's giving ten cents of every dollar you have to help some good cause. For years, Miss Chrissman has been saving her money, ten cents by ten cents. Now she has enough to help educate some Negro."

"Me?" asked Mary.

"Yes, you."

"I don't understand," said Mary. "Miss Chrissman doesn't know me. She has never even heard of me."

"No, but I have." Miss Wilson smiled at her favorite pupil. "Miss Chrissman wrote to Scotia Seminary in Concord, North Carolina, where I went to school. She said she'd like to give a scholarship for a Negro girl."

"What's a scholarship?" asked Mary.

"It's money for somebody's education."

"Did Scotia Seminary say I could have it?"

Miss Wilson said, "They told me I could have it to give to some girl in Mayesville Institute. They said that I must pick one that would be likely to do well."

"And you picked my Mary?" Patsy tried hard to keep back her tears. "But how'll she get to Scotia? We've no money."

"Here's her railroad ticket." Miss Wilson handed it to Patsy.

Again Mary fell on her knees. "Lord," she prayed, "I thank you and Miss Chrissman. And I promise, Lord, that I'll always try to share what I learn with other Negro girls."

Everyone was very proud of Mary. Friends made dresses and knitted stockings for her. The storekeeper gave her a pair of new shoes. When the day came for her to get on a train and go a hundred and fifty miles, a neighbor drove her to the station so she wouldn't have to walk on such an important day.

Miss Wilson was there to see Mary off. Just before Mary got on the train, Miss Wilson put a beautiful warm shawl around her shoulders. "It'll be colder in Concord," she said.

"And be sure to write, Mary. I'll take your letters out and read them to your mother."

"And you write to me."

"I will," Miss Wilson promised.

Mary's car was right behind the engine and it got all the smoke that puffed out. The whistle blew. Mary's friends hurried off the train. She pressed her nose against the dirty car window and waved goodbye to her neighbors and her family and to her childhood.

She didn't have time to become sad because she was too interested in the train. She sat on a fancy red plush seat which prickled even through her knitted wool stockings. Above her was a curving shiny ceiling. The window through which she looked was bigger than any she had ever seen.

She gave her ticket to the conductor. "Goin' to Concord all by yourself?" he asked.

"Yes, Sir," she said. "To Scotia Seminary."

Mary watched the country slide by her window. How big it was! It was America. There were cotton fields like hers. She was glad she wasn't working in one of them. There were trees and flowers she could name. Just like those on the road to Mayesville.

When Mary finally felt hungry she unwrapped the lunch that had been made at home.

She hadn't intended to speak to anyone on the train. Miss Wilson had told her not to. But she just couldn't help saying to an old woman across the aisle, "Look! A

33

whole half chicken! I never had a breast before—just necks and wings."

The old lady smiled and took her own thick sandwich out of a paper bag.

Four

Eight hours after she had left Mayesville, Mary stepped off the train at Concord, North Carolina. She felt lonely as she watched the train puff away.

The only other person on the platform was a white woman. She held out her hand and said, "Are you Mary McLeod?"

Mary said, "Yes, Ma'am."

"I've come to meet you."

Mary could hardly believe her ears. Why had this white lady with the nice smile come to meet her? Why should she bother about her?

The lady explained that she was a teacher at Scotia Seminary. Her home was in Boston, but she had come here to teach because she wanted to help give Negro girls a chance to learn.

Mary Jane thought, "She would never say in a horrid tone to anyone, 'You can't read.'"

Being met and taken to the school by a white woman was the first of many surprises for Mary Jane.

For the first time in her life she climbed stairs. The one floor of the four-room McLeod cabin had squatted close to the ground. Mary followed the white teacher who led her upstairs.

The room itself was a surprise. Never had Mary shared a room with only one person. At home many of the seventeen children slept in one room. Mary's room-

mate's name was Abby Greely. She had
been at Scotia two years and she helped
Mary become accustomed to her new
life. Mary liked her and the girls re-
mained friends all their lives.

Mary had never had a single bed. She
had never had a desk all her own. She
had never had a bureau all to herself, nor
a special chair.

The teacher told Mary to wash and
come down to the dining room for supper. In front of Mary was still another
surprise. There was a wash basin and
pitcher just for her. She thought of the
one tub on the porch at home. She
laughed when she remembered how she
had to fight each morning to get a chance
to wash in it.

In the dining room Mary saw black
teachers and white teachers eating together at the same table. For the first
time she ate at a table spread with a
white table cloth. She saw other girls use
napkins. She watched them and then un-

folded her napkin and spread it in her lap. She used a fork for the first time. The McLeods had only spoons and knives.

Miss Chrissman's scholarship money didn't pay Mary's whole bill at Scotia. She needed to earn more. At the school she cooked. She polished glass lamp chimneys until they shone. She scrubbed floors and kept the stairs swept and dusted. Patsy had taught her to iron and she did this so well, she was paid to iron shirts for Dr. Satterfield, the principal.

Besides her chores at the school, Mary worked in the homes of white families in Concord.

She worked in nearby tobacco fields almost as hard as she had worked in her home cotton fields. Everywhere she worked, people praised her. They said to each other, "Scotia must be a pretty good school if girls like Mary go there."

Her teachers said she "established good relations between the town and the school." Mary wasn't quite sure what

40

"good relations" meant but she was sure her teachers approved of them.

Besides finding many new situations at Scotia, Mary learned some things about herself. She had always liked to sing but never realized there was anything special about her voice. At Scotia she took singing lessons and her teachers said she had an unusually deep, contralto voice. When she sang in the school choir in Faith Hall, people said the music sounded better. Mary loved to sing in Faith Hall with its stained-glass windows.

Mary went to a class in public speaking which she liked immediately. If her audience didn't agree with her, she wasn't afraid to argue with them. "You have a logical mind and dramatic forcefulness," one teacher told her.

"What does that mean?" Mary asked.

"It means you can think straight. You can say what you think and make it interesting."

Her schoolmates thought so too. They loved to get her up on a rainbarrel to make speeches. Many times she spoke about Negroes.

While Mary was at Scotia, she thought a great deal about her own race. Where did Negroes come from? Africa, of course. Why were they in America where most people were white? Why had they been slaves? Why did Lincoln free them?

She wondered about these things. Then she learned how to find books in the library that would answer her questions.

She read about "inalienable rights" in the Declaration of Independence. What did "inalienable" mean? She looked it up in a dictionary in the library. It meant "that which cannot be taken away."

Abraham Lincoln had known that. Freedom had been taken away from Africans in America. He gave it back to them with the Emancipation Proclamation.

Mary had always known about that. It had made Patsy and Sam free.

Somewhere she had read that the home of the Negro race was called *darkest* Africa because it needed enlightenment. Missionaries had tried to bring that light. Mary thought about this for a long time. Then she decided she would be a missionary.

She went to the principal. "I want to go to Africa—to be a missionary."

"You're sure?" Dr. Satterfield asked.

"Yes."

"Then the place to go is Moody Institute in Chicago. I'll try to get you a scholarship."

"I'll write to them tonight too," Mary said.

She got an answer soon. She could come. Miss Chrissman thought she had done so well at Scotia that she would help her at Moody Institute with another scholarship.

Mary had been at Scotia seven years—

two years more than most of her class-
mates. During that time she had taken ad-
vanced courses. A missionary should know
a great deal.

Standing on the platform on Commencement Day, she was, as Granny had
said, "No-wise pretty." She was short and
big-boned, but people who heard her
said she was electric. She had a spark
about her.

After commencement Mary went home
for a short visit. She wanted to see her
family before she went to Chicago and
none of them could afford to attend her
graduation.

She had saved enough money from odd
jobs to buy her ticket home. She bought
presents for her father and mother—
slippers for Sam and a dozen tin forks for
Patsy. She was almost afraid to give her
mother the forks. Suppose it looked as if
she had become "uppity," too good to sop
up gravy with a piece of bread? Suppose

they thought her too fine to eat pork with her fingers?

She needn't have worried. Patsy was delighted with her gift. She showed the forks to all her neighbors. Many of them headed for the store to buy some for themselves. The supply at the store ran out.

Many Negro friends dropped by to ask the "educated McLeod girl" all sorts of questions. The young girls wanted to know how to trim their hats and how to fix their hair. The mothers had heard it was a good idea to boil drinking water. Was it?

One night each week Mary invited the neighbors to come to a class at the McLeod cabin. She read stories and poetry. They all sang hymns and spirituals.

On Sunday she put new life into the Sunday school.

While Mary was at home, she pitched in with the cotton picking. For the first time in her life she beat her father at it.

Five

———————————————————

~~~~~~

After several weeks at home it was time for her to leave. Again her friends helped her into the car with her baggage. The train pulled away from the station. This time it was taking Mary far, far away to Chicago.

Mary was the only Negro at Moody Institute except one student from Africa. However, there were other dark-skinned people from China, India, Japan. This mixture of colors didn't trouble Mary. She said, "In my heart I feel no difference between the white man or the black man or the yellow man or the brown man."

The teachers at Moody Institute soon discovered Mary's fine voice and made her a member of the Gospel Choir Team. That group went out on the Gospel Train to teach and preach and sing. Mary had a chance to ride through Illinois, Lincoln's state, and through other Northern states. She sang and talked in many little towns where the children had never seen a Negro or yellow-skinned Chinese. They didn't know what to make of this dark lady who sang so beautifully.

In one home where she visited the little daughter clung to her. Dinner time came. Mary was invited to the table. She started toward it.

Evidently the little girl had been taught that she herself could not come to the table without washing her hands. She said, "Mother, make her wash her hands. They're dirty."

The mother was embarrassed. But Mary laughed. She said to the little girl, "Here, feel my face, then let me feel yours."

The child gently rubbed the skin that looked like dark velvet. Mary smoothed the peach-pink cheeks. They looked at their hands. Mary said, "See. I didn't come off on your hands and you didn't come off on mine." They laughed.

Mary said, "I like the skin God gave me and I like yours too."

When Mary got back from one trip on the Gospel Train, there was bad news from home. Her parents' cabin had burned down. This was worse than the death of the mule. A cabin cost much money. She hadn't any to send Sam and Patsy. What could she do? She just must earn something to send to them.

A few days later she thought of something. She sang before a meeting of white women who gave her forty dollars. That was a good deal of money in those days, and Mary sent all of it to Sam and Patsy. It helped them start building a new cabin. For years after she continued sending them money whenever she could.

As soon as Mary was graduated from Moody Institute she took a long train trip to New York. She went to the Presbyterian Board of Missions. She hoped that her years and good grades at Moody would prove that she was ready to become a missionary. But this time going to the head men didn't work. She was told she was too young.

Later Mary said it was the cruelest disappointment of her life. What should she do now?

There seemed to be nothing to do but go home to Mayesville. She'd have to tell her family she couldn't be a missionary in darkest Africa. She'd have to tell Miss

Wilson, Miss Chrissman, and Dr. Satterfield.

Sally, her married sister, and her baby were visiting at home when Mary arrived.

Sally said, "Never did see any sense in going to Africa. Better get a job in Mayesville."

"You let Mary alone," scolded her mother. "The Lord's prob'ly got big plans for her someday."

"Someday, someday, someday," said Sally. "Mary always had the 'somedays.' Now you got 'em."

Again Mary helped in the cotton picking.

It was nearly November when the picking was finished. It was time for school to begin. To her surprise, Mary found that it wouldn't begin for two months. The Negroes in the neighborhood had decided their "kids didn't need so much schoolin'." The teacher wasn't coming yet.

Mary couldn't stand that. What if some child wanted school as much as she had? She went to every house where there were Negro children. She told them to be in school the first Monday in November. She would be there too, she promised. She wasn't sure they would come, but she was going to be there!

As she stood in the doorway and looked out, she saw about twenty children in the school yard. She rang the bell, and they came in and took seats. Mary looked at the girl who sat in her old seat. Sure enough! The chair was too high and the desk was too low. She'd have to double up to write just as Mary had. When the room was quiet, Mary said, "Good morning, children. I'm *Miss* McLeod."

She taught the school until Miss Wilson came. She liked to teach. Now she knew she wanted to do it all her life.

She wrote to the Board of Missions to

ask for a job and they wrote that a teacher was needed in Augusta, Georgia, at the Haines Normal Institute. The principal was Miss Lucy Laney.

Six

Lucy Laney, twenty years older than Mary, was the founder of the school. She had been born a slave. Fortunately she had always been treated kindly by her owner. That lady had taught Lucy to read and had allowed her to use the books in her own library.

Lucy, like Mary, had always wanted to do something for her race. She did something very worthwhile for Mary. She helped her to see that Africans in America needed attention just as Negroes in Africa did. She made Mary feel better about being too young to go to Africa as a missionary.

When Lucy had started her school for black children in Augusta, Georgia, she gave the small school a big name—The Haines Normal and Industrial Institute. The first year the school was in the basement of a church. The next year Lucy managed to pay the rent on a deserted house and barn. Nobody would live in the house. It was supposed to be haunted. And the barn was too close to it for comfort.

Her work there was so successful that the Presbyterian Mission in the North sent her $10,000. Soon a wealthy man gave her a piece of land. Another man gave her enough money to build a brick building.

It was in this building that Mary began to teach. She also lived in the building.

From her window she looked down on a neighborhood called "The Terry." Why it was called that she never knew. The houses were poor and tumbledown. Swarming out of them came unruly, dirty children. They kicked up clouds of dust in dry weather and wallowed in mud when the streets were wet after a rain. Nobody seemed to pay any attention to them.

That was too much for Mary. She couldn't watch from her window and do nothing to help. She asked Miss Laney, "May I ask them to come to our school on Sunday afternoons?"

Miss Laney said, "Yes."

So Mary went out into The Terry, inviting every child she met to come to the school.

A few came, looking tough and ready to make trouble. But Mary knew that most Negro children liked to sing. She selected songs they knew and she began to sing. Soon everybody was singing with her. Later she told them Bible stories.

The word went around the neighborhood that Sundays at the school were fun. More and more children came until sometimes there were nearly a thousand, standing, sitting, crowding. All were singing lustily with Mary's contralto voice loudest and sweetest of all.

After a few years the Presbyterian Board which had sent Mary to Haines Institute instead of to Africa, sent her to other schools in the South. One of them was Kendall Institute in Sumter, South Carolina. At Kendall she met and married Albertus Bethune who was teaching there. Later he taught in Savannah, Georgia. There Mary's only son, Albert, was born.

Having a child of her own made Mary more anxious than ever to help make the America she loved a better place for Negroes. She was sure that the best way to do that was to have a school of her own.

She thought and thought about it. What kind of school should it be? Where should it be? How could she get the money for it? She thought about how, long ago, little Mary Jane McLeod, working in the cotton fields, had prayed for a chance to "get educated." Her prayer had been answered. Now Mary McLeod Bethune prayed to be shown how to start a school to educate other Negro children.

She and her husband moved to Palatka, Florida, where he had a new teaching position.

Seven

~~~~~~

Henry Flagler was building a railroad all the way down the east coast of Florida, from Jacksonville to Miami. He was employing Negro workers because they were cheap. A great many of them were in Daytona. Most of them had children. They were living in shacks worse than those in The Terry in Augusta. The children were running wild in the streets. Mary seemed to hear a voice say, "That is the place. Build your school there."

Besides the laborers at Daytona, many rich white people came there for the winter. Mary had faith that somehow she could get help from them. She remembered the generous men who had helped Miss Laney build her school in Augusta.

Her husband, Albertus, wasn't so sure about her school. He thought Palatka was a pretty good place for them to live. He reminded her that they had very little money—only a dollar and fifty cents. She couldn't start a school with that. Besides, where would she get her pupils?

Mary listened but she never gave up her idea. She knew that if she went to Daytona, Albertus would come too.

One day she begged a ride for herself and her little boy with a family that was going to Daytona. It was only seventy miles away. But in 1904 the sand was deep on Florida roads. Practically no one had an automobile—certainly not the poor family that gave Mary and little Albert a ride. So it was three dusty days after they left Palatka before they reached Daytona. There Mary hunted up the only person she knew and she and little Albert stayed with this friend a few days.

As she had done in The Terry in Augusta, Mary walked up and down the poor streets of Daytona. She was looking for two things—a building for the school she was determined to start and some pupils for that school.

After a day or two, she found an empty shack on Oak Street. She thought this would do. The owner said she could rent it for $11.00 a month. But it wasn't worth that much. The paint had peeled off, the front steps wobbled so that she had to hang onto the shaky railing to keep from falling, the house was dirty, it had a leaky roof. In most of the windows the panes of glass were broken or cracked.

Eleven dollars a month! Mary said she had only $1.50. She promised to pay the rent as soon as she could earn the money.

The owner trusted her. By the time she was sure she could have the building, she had five little girls from the neighborhood as her pupils.

What a school! A rickety old house and five little girls!

The little girls pitched in and cleaned the house. The neighbors helped with scrubbing brushes, brooms, hammers, nails and saws. Soon the cottage could be lived in, but there were no chairs, no tables, no beds. There was no stove. However there were no pots and pans to cook in even if there had been a stove.

Mary set about changing these things. She found things in trash piles and the city dump. Nobody but Mrs. Bethune would have thought of making tables and chairs and desks from the old crates she picked up and brought home. Behind the hotels on the beach she found cracked dishes, old lamps, even some old clothes. She took them home too. Everything was scoured and mended and used. "Keep

things clean and neat" was her motto then; and as long as she lived the pupils in her school had to live up to that motto. She found a piece of gay cretonne and made a ruffled skirt of it to brighten up the packing box she used for her own desk.

Her little pupils had no pencils. They wrote with charcoal slivers made from burned logs. Their ink was elderberry juice. What good was ink or a pencil if there was no paper to write on? Mrs. Bethune took care of that too.

Every time she went to the store to get a little food, or a few pots and pans, she had each article wrapped separately. The pieces of wrapping paper were carefully removed and smoothed out. The little girls used this paper to write their lessons with their charcoal pencils.

She needed a cook stove very badly but she couldn't pay for one. What should she do? Her little pupils had to have warm food.

Unexpectedly, the problem was solved for her. One day a wrinkled old white neighbor said to her, "Can you read?"

Mary said, "Yes."

"Then will you read me this letter from my son? I just can't find my glasses."

Mary picked up the letter from the table. Under it lay the lost glasses.

"Poor thing," thought Mary. "She just pretends she can read."

She read the letter to her.

"Thanks," said the mother.

Mary turned to go. "You're welcome."

The old woman stood by her open door and thought a moment. Then she said, "I got an old cook stove. 'Taint doin' me a mite o' good. Would you want it?"

Mary certainly did want it. She needed it to cook food for her five little girls. Soon it did much more.

It was October 3, 1904, that Mary Bethune opened her school. She gave it a long name, Daytona Educational and Industrial Training School for Negro Girls. That was an even longer name than Lucy Laney had given her school in Augusta.

Mary's $1.50 was spent. She had to have more money. The parents of her five little girls were able to pay her only fifty cents a week.

Again Mary walked the streets near her school asking questions. She found that many of the families had poor food. The men who weren't married were especially in need of good food. What was better than a sweet potato pie? And who could bake a better pie than Mary Bethune? Nobody. Mary set her girls to work peeling sweet potatoes. She baked the pies in her new stove and sold them to the workmen. Word got around to the winter visitors that Mary Bethune's sweet potato pies were the best ever. Some of the white ladies came to sample them. They always bought a great many.

Mary began to wonder what other Southern treat she and her girls could sell to these people from the North. She had heard that they liked Negro music, especially spirituals, so she trained her little girls to sing together and took them to the big hotels.

Eight

At one of the hotels she met a very rich man named Henry Kaiser. He liked the concert she and her girls gave and a few days later he took the singers in his boat to the Ormand Hotel, a few miles away. There they sang for another rich man, John D. Rockefeller. That was a lucky day. Mr. Rockefeller liked their music. He gave each child a shiny new dime. Better still, he gave the school an organ.

That was only one of the many gifts he kept giving.

One customer for Mary's pies was James A. Gamble, the soap manufacturer of Cincinnati, Ohio. Mr. Gamble's firm made Ivory Soap. By the time Mary knew him she was already dreaming of owning land on which she would build her own schoolhouse. It would be much better than the shack she was renting. She asked Mr. Gamble to be a trustee of her school.

She told her son, and Albert asked, "What's a trustee?"

"A person who helps get money for a school and helps make the rules," Mary explained.

She invited Mr. Gamble to come see her.

One day he drove out. All he saw was the old unpainted cottage on the edge of a dump heap. It didn't look like any school he had ever seen.

"Where is the school you want me to be a trustee for?" he asked.

"In my mind," said Mary.

He laughed. "I'll come back next winter," he said and he gave her a check for a hundred dollars.

Mary thanked him and hoped her mind would work fast before next winter.

One day not long after that a man stopped her on the street. She was riding her bicycle.

"Didn't I hear the little girls from your school sing at my hotel the other night?"

Mary was glad to tell him that he did. She remembered seeing him in the audience.

"I'd like to see your school," he said. "Get into the car and let me take you home." He boosted her bicycle in too.

He, like Mr. Gamble, was surprised to see that the school was only a little shack. He saw a girl trying to sew on a broken-down sewing machine. That was too much for him. For he was Thomas White, manufacturer of the White sewing

81

machine. The next day he sent Mrs. Bethune and her girls a new White machine with all the latest attachments. After that he gave them many other gifts and much money. When he died a number of years later, he left the school enough money to build a big assembly hall. It was finished in 1916 and was named White Hall.

Mr. White, Mr. Gamble, and a number of other rich men told Mary they would all like to be trustees of the new school she had in her mind. They believed in what she was trying to do—to make a better life for the people of her race. They had faith in her.

She made them laugh with the story of how she had bought the old dump behind her little cottage. It was the land on which she hoped to build a bigger and better school. Those trustees were all smart businessmen. They liked a bargain. Mary told them that the owner of the land had told her that his price was $1,000. A thousand dollars! It wasn't worth it. And even if it were, where would she get the money?

"I don't suppose you know this, Sir," she said, "but people around here call this land of yours 'Hell's Hole.' Full of mosquitoes, weeds, and snakes the way it is, I'm not sure it's good for anything."

Mary got the land for $200 instead of $1,000. The owner said she could pay it five dollars at a time. She didn't tell him she didn't have even the first five dollars. He would have worried, but Mary Bethune had faith in God and in herself. She even had faith in sweet potato pies. She knew she could sell as many as she could bake.

Her friends and neighbors cleared the swamp for her. At night the sky was bright from the big bonfires they built of the rubbish. They planted blooming shrubs and other flowers where only weeds had been.

One space they left bare. On it Mrs.

Bethune planned to put a building big enough for her growing school.

She knew she would need a great deal of money for the school. Her wealthy trustees might help, but she must get more money. She wrote letters to many people to get them interested and she went to businessmen.

By 1907 Mary had enough money to finish her wooden building. She named it Faith Hall. Years later friends helped her replace it with a fireproof brick structure— still called Faith Hall.

Across the street from Faith Hall the girls raised vegetables. Some of their customers not only bought vegetables but they also brought presents to the school. One gave them three pigs.

When Booker T. Washington visited the school, he said to Mary, "I'm glad you have pigs. They never fail you. Feed 'em, fatten 'em, sell 'em, and then buy more."

One Sunday Mary and some of her pupils went for a picnic in the nearby Piney Woods. There, at a place called Tomoka, turpentine was made from the sap of the pine trees. Mrs. Bethune was very much upset when she saw how the families of the men who worked in the pine forest lived. It was a disgrace.

When Mary Bethune got mad, things happened. Things began to happen then. Mary taught the women how to clean up their filthy homes. She brought them medicine for the sick. She started a school for the children. After a few years she had started five mission schools. On Sundays she invited everybody to come and sing. Crowds came, as they had come from The Terry to Haines Institute.

During the years that she was opening these schools she did not neglect Bethune Institute. She kept planning and working for it. A hospital was built. She named it McLeod Hospital in memory of her father who had died a few years earlier.

For one of the few times in her life,

Mary spent some money for her own pleasure. She bought a railroad ticket and sent it to her mother. Patsy, seventy years old and still carrying herself like a queen, took her first train trip. Mary showed her mother all around her school. Did her mother think, as she looked around the campus, that the first step toward building this wonderful school was taken the day Mary trudged off to Miss Wilson's school to learn to read?

It was very pleasant and exciting to Mary Bethune to see building after building go up on her campus. But other things happened that were frightening.

One dark night the Ku Klux Klan, its members wearing white sheets and carrying blazing torches, visited the school.

They looked like ghosts coming up the steps of a building. They didn't like the way Mary had been telling the Negroes they should vote. Of course she told them to vote. Why shouldn't she? It was their right. The Klansmen thought they could scare her but they didn't know her very well. She stood on the steps, between two white pillars, and faced them. She wore a long flowing cape. She looked as queenly as her mother. Light from the hall shone out on her. Every window was lighted. In the building the choir she had trained was practicing. Eighty men from the Ku Klux Klan faced her.

"We'll burn your buildings if you keep teaching these people of yours they can vote."

Just then the choir sang loudly, cheerfully, "Be not dismayed, whate'r betide God will take care of you."

Mrs. Bethune nodded her head as though she were agreeing with them. She stood as tall as she could. She wished she were five feet ten inches instead of only five feet two or three inches. She was very angry but she said quietly, "If you burn them, I'll build them up again."

The men backed away. In their haste one of them dropped a full can of kerosene. Quick as a flash, the school's night watchman darted out the door and picked it up.

"You can use this kerosene," he said to Mrs. Bethune.

The next morning a procession of Negroes marched up to the voting place. Mrs. Bethune led them. Many of them voted for the first time. The story of how a Negro schoolteacher in Florida had stood up to the Ku Klux Klan was told in the newspapers all over America.

Nine

In the year 1923 Mrs. Bethune decided that her school should be open to boys as well as girls. To be sure, there were four or five little boys there but they needed company. She liked what she knew about a boys' school in Jacksonville, Florida. It was called Cookman Institute. The Methodist Episcopal Church owned it. Mary talked over a plan with the church authorities, and finally she came to an agreement with them. She gave the school over to the church. They had to raise the money to keep it going. Mary's days of begging for her school were over. The new school was called Bethune-Cookman College. Mary was the president. She decided what was to be taught.

Some of the boys thought that life would be pretty soft and easy in a school with a woman president. They soon found out how wrong they were. They discovered it wasn't healthy to be late. Mary began everything on time—classes, meals, games.

The students did not leave their rooms dirty or untidy. Nobody ever knew when President Bethune would appear on the campus in a *white* dress. When she did, look out! Anybody who had left an untidy room had better scamper. The lady in white was on an inspection tour. She would look into every dusty corner and examine every badly made bed. Clothes had to be hanging in closets, and not be jammed in a pile on the floor.

The girls continued to learn housekeeping. The boys had shop work and manual training. Both boys and girls had regular high school studies. Mary didn't want any of her children to be unprepared for college.

Above all, both boys and girls had to be taught good citizenship.

Mary tacked up mottoes on the walls of the schoolrooms. One came from the memory of the little white girls who had so cruelly told her, "You can't read." It was, "Blessed is he that readeth." In the kitchen the girls saw the motto, "Cease to be a drudge, seek to be an artist."

An artist in the kitchen? How could that be?

"Make every dish you serve, every cake you bake look pretty as well as taste good," they were told.

Not having to raise money for her school took a load off of Mary's fifty-year-old shoulders. She had been carrying that load alone since her husband had died in 1919. Her son, Albert, was now a grown man with his own life to live. Perhaps now she could rest a little. Rest? Friends saw to it that she did better than that. She could have a good time with no money worries. For eight weeks she could just "pleasure herself." Where? In Europe. All her expenses were paid by her friends.

She went to London, Paris, and Rome. In Rome the Pope gave her his blessing.

Italy was the nearest she ever came to Africa, where she had once hoped to go as a missionary.

When she got back to New York, she had the great pleasure of meeting Mrs. Franklin D. Roosevelt. It was at a luncheon at the home of her mother-in-law, Mrs. James Roosevelt. Some of the white women from the South who were also guests raised their eyebrows. At home they didn't eat lunch with a black person even if she was famous. Eleanor Roosevelt sat next to Mary. That day began a lasting friendship. The women spoke at meetings together often.

Ten

Eleanor Roosevelt's husband became
President of the United States in a period
known as "the depression years." Many
people were miserably poor. There was
little work to be had. Young and old
needed relief.

Mary went about the country making
speeches, trying to help. She felt that her
audiences would "pay her more mind" if
she could say to them. "I'm not speaking

as Mary Bethune. I am the voice of the colored women of America—800,000 of them." Eight hundred thousand! That was the number of women in the National Council of Negro Women which Mary had organized. It was an impressive group.

Before long they decided that they needed a clubhouse. They found a house in Washington, D.C.

"We can't ever afford that," they said to Mary.

"Oh, yes we can—someday." She laughed. "There, I've got the 'somedays' again. That's what my sister used to call my impossible ideas."

In a year they had the house. The women themselves raised as much money as they could. Mary used her old plan for getting money. Find a rich man. Make him believe in what you want. Ask him for the money you need. Thank him, and walk away with his check. This time the man was Marshall Field, the rich merchant of Chicago. She went out of his office with a check for $10,000, and the National Council of Negro Women had a home. There Mrs. Bethune could consult with other leaders about what to say when she spoke for them. She went talking, talking, talking all over the nation.

In 1935 there were over two million young people between sixteen and twenty-four out of work. One of them was asked, "If you haven't been at work, what have you been doing? How do you spend your time?"

"What is there to do?" He had little hope.

They lined up on fences beside the road and talked or just swung their feet. Some of them sold apples on street corners.

To help them President Roosevelt set up an organization. It was called the National Youth Administration. It was usually spoken of as the N.Y.A. The President asked Mary to be on its Advisory Board, and she accepted.

The Board's plan gave almost every one of the unemployed youths 44.5 hours work a week. Their average wage was $15.73 per month. It wasn't much, but it was better than nothing. The boys did building and farming; they did all sorts of work in city parks. Both boys and girls who had a little education worked in public libraries. They became stenographers and clerks. The girls worked in nursery schools and at lunch counters.

Mary worked hard to make sure that as many Negro young people as possible could have work.

After a year she went to the White House to give the President a report. She talked from her heart. "Negro boys and girls have worked hard for some education. Now they can't use it. There are no jobs for them. Oh, maybe a few at ten or fifteen dollars a month. You've got to do

better than that for my people, Mr. President."

Suddenly she thought in horror, "I'm lecturing the President of the United States. You'd think he was one of my pupils!"

She sank back into her chair. She wondered if she had ruined everything. But a few weeks later she was asked to take a new position in the N.Y.A. It was Director of Minority Affairs.

This meant that Mary would have to help many more people than just her fellow Negroes. These included black people, yellow people, brown people, and foreign white people.

At first she said, "I can't possibly do it. I must look after my college." Friends said, "You *must* do it. This is the first time a Negro woman has ever been offered such a post."

Mary accepted. She was now over sixty years old. In her new position she traveled 3,500 miles a year, and she visited and spoke in twenty states.

She overworked, and the attacks of asthma, which had long troubled her, became worse. She had to have an operation. While at Johns Hopkins Hospital in Baltimore she kept a daily record. She told of the huge baskets of flowers Mrs. Roosevelt sent twice a week from the White House. She wrote about the strict diet they put her on to reduce her weight.

She appreciated the good care the nurses gave her, but she never allowed them to call her "Mary." "I am *Mrs.* Bethune," she said. Her memory of *Miss* Wilson had never died.

On December 7, 1941, the Japanese dropped a surprise bomb on Pearl Harbor in the Hawaiian Islands. Mary Bethune sprang into action—ready to serve wherever her country needed her. "I am my mother's daughter," she said. "The drums of Africa still beat in my heart. They will not let me rest."

Her work with the N.Y.A. was over. In the spring after Pearl Harbor, Congress created the Women's Army Training Corps. W.A.C. it was called. Everything had initials in those days. The American Council of Negro Women asked the Secretary of War to appoint Mary Bethune Assistant Director. Mrs. Oveta Culp Hobby of Texas was Director. Mrs. Bethune worried for fear this white Southern woman might not want to give black girls a chance to serve as officers. She need not have been fearful. Mrs. Hobby was as anxious as she was to see that Negro girls received the same treatment as whites. They were in separate units from the white girls, but that was an army regulation.

Again Mary went across the country. Again bad health slowed her down. She had to give up something. Should it be the presidency of Bethune-Cookman Col-

lege, the presidency of the National
Council of Negro Women, or the Direc-
torship of the W.A.C.? What a problem!

She decided that more people in the
United States depended on her in the
W.A.C and in the National Council of
Negro Women than in her beloved col-
lege.

The college now had nearly twenty
buildings and over thirty teachers. There
were almost seven hundred students instead of five little girls. It had an "A"
rating among Negro colleges of the
South. She hated to resign as its president. It was her "baby." She must have
felt like a mother giving up her child. But
she did resign. How she would have liked
to set her sixty-five-year-old self down in
a comfortable chair in her cottage on the
edge of the campus and let other people
do the work of the world and the war!

If she had done that, she would not
have been Mary McLeod Bethune. She

would not have been Patsy's little Mary
who was "somehow different."

She kept her house on the campus although she continued her war work. She
spent much of her time in Washington.
Her constant letter writing to her "children" in the service was as important as
anything she did. No letter from a troubled boy or girl anywhere went unan-
swered. Nobody knows how many boys
and girls wrote to her. Boys wrote, "You
are my pin-up girl." A white-haired girl
with a jet black face. This was the girl
whose grandmother had long ago said,
"She's no-wise pretty." She was a strange
pin-up girl in an army barracks!

Again she started out over the country.
She hammered on one idea—Negroes
must have equal rights with white people. She was nearing her seventieth birth-
day. She walked with a cane which she
said she carried for "swank." Her
speeches were as electric as they had

been at Scotia Seminary. People listened.

On April 12, 1945, she was in Dallas, Texas, when news came that President Roosevelt had died in Warm Springs, Georgia. She flew at once to Washington, and in the White House she wept with others at the loss of a good friend.

What were her thoughts as she sat in that quiet room? Did she remember how he had said to her, "I always like to see you, Mrs. Bethune. You never ask for anything for yourself. Always for others."

In April, 1945, two weeks after the President's death, people from many countries met in San Francisco to form the United Nations and to write its charter. Eleanor Roosevelt had insisted that Mary Bethune be there to speak for her race.

These two friends had a quiet talk together and Mrs. Bethune reminded Mrs. Roosevelt that her husband had said she never wanted anything for herself. "Now I am asking. I should like something that belonged to President Roosevelt." Mrs. Roosevelt gave her his gold-headed cane. She never walked without it.

Eleven

In 1949 the trustees of Rollins College in Winter Park, Florida, asked Mary to accept an honorary degree.

Mary Bethune received the first honorary degree ever given to a Negro by a white Southern college.

She stood as tall as she could as she listened to President Holt say, "Mary McLeod Bethune, I deem it one of the highest privileges that has come to me as

President of Rollins College to do honor
to you this morning. I am proud that
Rollins is, I am told, the first white college in the South to bestow an honorary
degree on one of your race. You have in
your own person demonstrated that from
the humblest beginnings and through the
most adverse circumstances it is still possible for one who has the will, the intelli-
gence, the courage, and the never-failing
faith in God and in your fellowman to
rise from the humblest cabin in the land
to a place of honor and influence among
the world's eminent. In paying honor to
you we again show our own faith in the
land which made your career a reality."

Then the Dean of the College put
around her shoulders a kind of cape
called a doctor's hood. Its lining was blue
and gold, the colors of Rollins College.
There was an outer band of white velvet
which meant Mary was now a Doctor of
Humanities.

Mary Bethune, the best cotton-picker

in the McLeod family, the President of Bethune-Cookman College, walked slowly down the aisle of the chapel. In front of her and behind her were other new Doctors, wearing their blue-and-gold hoods, but all of them were white.

At another time in that same year, the college had given the same degree to President Harry S. Truman. He had walked down the chapel aisle wearing the same kind of blue-and-gold-lined hood.

Although her health was not good, Mary continued helping a cause she had always fought for—equal schooling for Negroes and whites.

In 1954 she was seventy-nine years old; her school was fifty years old. It made her very happy when in that year the Supreme Court of the United States announced the decision that all schools must be open to every child of every color.

Mary Bethune knew that could not happen right away, but it did not dim her happiness as she sailed across the campus, swinging her Roosevelt cane. "Sing," she commanded the students. She led them with her strong beautiful voice.

A year later Mary Bethune died.

Her spirit is still there in her house on the corner of her campus.

It is called The Mary Bethune Foundation now. The living room has the same furniture she used. Near the door is a trophy case with her many medals.

Her desk is as she left it. It almost seems as if she might walk in and sit in the chair behind it.

Across the narrow hall is a bedroom. On the footboard of the bed is a neat notice which says that Eleanor Roosevelt once slept there.

In 1960, Congress passed a bill stating that a stone monument was to be erected to Mary Bethune. It was to be placed in a public place in Washington. Never before had such a monument been placed in the Nation's Capital for a Negro woman.

It was appropriate that members of the

National Council of Negro Women asked that the stone monument be unveiled January 1, 1963—the one-hundredth anniversary of Lincoln's Emancipation Proclamation which set Sam and Patsy McLeod free from slavery. As this book went to press the stone had not been erected, but the National Council of Negro Women has been called Mary Bethune's *living* monument.